The Institute for Priestly Formation

Mission Statement

The Institute for Priestly Formation was founded to assist bishops in the spiritual formation of diocesan seminarians and priests in the Roman Catholic Church. The Institute responds to the need to foster spiritual formation as the integrating and governing principle of all aspects of priestly formation. Inspired by the biblical-evangelical spirituality of Ignatius Loyola, this spiritual formation has as its goal the cultivation of a deep interior communion with Christ; from such communion, the priest shares in Christ's own pastoral charity. In carrying out its mission, the Institute directly serves diocesan seminarians and priests, as well as those who are responsible for diocesan priestly formation.

The Institute for Priestly Formation
Creighton University
2500 California Plaza
Omaha, Neb., 68178
www.creighton.edu/ipf
ipf@creighton.edu

WRAP Yourself in Scripture

A Guide for *Lectio Divina*

Karen L. Dwyer, PhD | Lawrence A. Dwyer, JD

THE INSTITUTE FOR PRIESTLY FORMATION

IPF PUBLICATIONS

" The word of God is replete with manifold blessings, since it is, so to speak, a treasure of all goods. It is the source of faith, hope, charity, all virtues, all the gifts of the Holy Spirit, all the beatitudes of the Gospel, all good works, all the rewards of life, all the glory of paradise: Welcome the word that has taken root in you, with its power to save you. For the word of God is a light to the mind and a fire to the will. It enables man to know God and to love Him."

ST. LAWRENCE OF BRINDISI, Doctor of the Church
The Liturgy of the Hours, July 21, 1974

NIHIL OBSTAT: Father Michael F. Gutgsell
                 Censor Librorum,
                 December 13, 2005

IMPRIMATUR: Most Reverend Elden Francis Curtiss
                 Archbishop of Omaha
                 December 13, 2005

THE INSTITUTE FOR PRIESTLY FORMATION
IPF PUBLICATIONS
2500 California Plaza
Omaha, Nebraska 68178
www.IPFpublications.com

Printed in the United States of America
ISBN-13: 978-0-9843792-3-1
ISBN-10: 0-9843792-3-1

Table of Contents

Foreword

"Prayer is pure receptivity to God's grace, love in action, communion with the Spirit who dwells within us, leading us, through Jesus, in the Church, to our heavenly Father. In the power of his Spirit, Jesus is always present in our hearts, quietly waiting for us to be still with him to receive 'power from on high,' enabling us to be salt and light for our world" (World Youth Day, Randwick Racecourse, July 20, 2008). These words of Pope Benedict XVI invite us to discover new meaning in praying, especially praying with the Sacred Scriptures.

The Living Word of Sacred Scripture is ALIVE. Through *Lectio Divina* prayer (reading, meditating on, and praying Scripture), we exercise our hearts in faith and are drawn into tasting and seeing the very presence of God laboring in love for us.

WRAP, as explained in these pages, is a particularly anointed method of *Lectio Divina* prayer, and I recommend it. Through **WRAP**, we actually enter into the Heart of Jesus in the power of the Holy Spirit. In learning to practice **WRAP**, our hearts burn with healing love. The promises of Jesus' Heart – new life and new hope – become readily accessible as we learn to acknowledge, relate, receive, and respond to the Living Word in this highly personalized method of meditation and contemplative listening.

If you desire to exercise your spiritual senses to touch, taste, smell, feel and hear the utter nearness of the Word made flesh, Jesus' Risen Heart, you need only learn **WRAP** as a way of praying with the Bible. I want to encourage you to act on the desire to know and understand the love that lives in Jesus' Heart for you. But be prepared to ask for courage, which the Holy Spirit will gladly provide.

Encountering the Living Word through **WRAP** stretches us all to receive more love and grace than we ever thought or imagined possible. Through **WRAP**, our hearts receive a new ability to be grasped by the awesome mystery of the Trinity's love. **WRAP** provides us with a way of receiving practical counsel in the Holy Spirit, and a new intimate relationship with Jesus and the Father. This method of prayer will awaken your inner desire to become more and more "filled with all the fullness of God" **(Eph 3: 19)**.

May our Lord Jesus Christ bless you now with a new gift of reading and praying Scripture.

FATHER JOHN HORN, S. J., co-founder
The Institute for Priestly Formation, Omaha, Neb.

Introduction

You may wonder if God will ever speak to you or if He even wants to talk with you. The truth is: He does! *The Catechism of the Catholic Church* defines Christian prayer as "a covenant relationship between God and Man in Christ" (**CCC 2564**). Inherent in this relationship is a two-way conversation.

God desires to speak with you today, and His conversation goes quickly beyond the "Hi" or "How are you?" of a passing greeting. Too often, we either ignore conversation with Him, or we monopolize the conversation with only our concerns and needs.

God desires dialogue with you more than you could ever imagine. As the Second Vatican Council points out: "In the sacred books [of Scripture] the Father who is in heaven comes lovingly to meet his children and talks with them" (*Dei Verbum 21*).

This book is designed to help you converse with your Heavenly Father by learning a Scripture study method called **WRAP**.

WRAP is an acronym for a guided method of reading, reflecting on, and praying Holy Scripture. The goal of **WRAP** is to foster a personal encounter and conversation with Jesus Christ through the Scriptures. In a sense, **WRAP** is a way to help you feel "wrapped" in God's Word, as though you were wrapped in a garment of love and grace.

WRAP will lead you in developing a Scripture-based prayer life and encourage you to let the Word of God sink into your soul and spirit so that you no longer only see the words on a page but hear the words as God speaks to your heart.

Part I

Lectio Divina

"Above all it's the Gospels that occupy my mind when I'm in prayer, my poor soul has so many needs and yet this is the one thing needful. I'm always finding fresh lights there, hidden and enthralling meanings."

St. Therese of Lisieux, Doctor of the Church
Catechism of the Catholic Church, 127

Principles of *Lectio Divina*

WRAP is based on the principles of *Lectio Divina*, (pronounced Lect-see-oh Di-vee-na) an ancient, yet rediscovered, method of reading, reflecting on, and praying Scripture.

The Catechism of the Catholic Church describes *Lectio Divina* as a method "where the Word of God is so read and meditated on that it becomes prayer" (**CCC 1177**). This method has been practiced for centuries by the Desert Fathers, the Benedictines, the Carmelites, and various Doctors of the Church, including St. Gregory the Great, St. Jerome, St. John of the Cross, and St. Teresa of Avila, among others.

You do not have to be a Church doctor or live in a monastery to practice *Lectio Divina*. The benefits of reading, meditating on, and praying the Word of God are meant for all Christians. *Lectio Divina* is Latin for "divine reading" or "sacred reading" of Scripture.[1] It is much more than simply perusing the chapters of Scripture as if reading a novel or a newspaper. The Latin word *lectio* means deeply consuming a reading or teaching. Even the prophet Jeremiah wrote of devouring the Word of God into the depths of his being: "When I found your words, I devoured them; they became my joy and the happiness of my heart" (**Jer 15:16**).

The objective of *Lectio Divina* is to pay attention to God's Word so that a conversation develops between you and your Savior. By listening from the depths of your being with the help of the Holy Spirit, you will hear Christ speak to you in the once-hidden meaning of the verses of Scripture. Then you will speak with Jesus about these verses in relationship to the thoughts, feelings, and desires of your heart and the needs in your life.

Stages of *Lectio Divina*

Most biblical scholars list the four basic stages of *Lectio Divina* as **reading** (*Lectio*), **reflecting** (*Meditatio*), **praying** (*Oratio*), and **resting** (*Contemplatio*).

1. **Reading.** In *Lectio*, you read a passage of Scripture a few times and allow the words or verses to capture your attention. In this way, you begin to listen as God speaks to your heart.

2. **Reflecting.** In *Meditatio*, you reflect or meditate upon the words that caught your attention. In an effort to understand their meaning, you ponder and "chew on" them, seeking to acquire the mind of Christ and learning what He wants to reveal to you. In some passages, you may imagine yourself in the scene as an observer, reflecting on what you see, what you hear, and to whom you are drawn. You consider how the words you are reading relate to your life today.

3. **Praying.** In *Oratio*, you pray from your heart and respond to what Jesus has spoken to you in the words of Scripture. You allow the grace of the words to move you toward prayer. You personally ask Jesus for all the help and graces you need to respond to your reading and reflection. You have a conversation with your Lord.

4. **Resting.** In *Contemplatio*, you commune with God further and rest in His love and presence so that the very core of your being is stilled. Your attention is entirely centered on God. You allow the transformation process that the Word has stirred up to encourage, refresh, and strengthen you for a new level of beginning.[2]

Benefits of Praying Scripture

Several passages from Scripture itself encourage us to enter prayerful meditation. The word "meditate" means to reflect on, to contemplate, to ponder, to consider, to mull over, and to recite. Psalm 1:1-3 assures us that the one who finds "joy" in and meditates on Scripture day and night "prospers." This person gains strength, blessings on work, and fruitfulness, "like a tree planted near streams of water, that yields its fruit in season; its leaves never wither."

Hebrews 4:12 reminds us that "the word of God is living and effective." **It is life-changing** and can penetrate our being and shape our lives to the will of God. It is able to discern the "reflections and thoughts of the heart," even when we are unsure of them.

In Deuteronomy 6: 1-9, Moses exhorts the people to place the commands of God in their hearts, to teach those commands diligently to their children, and to apply those commands to their lives from morning until night in order to obtain a **blessed family life**.

In other Psalms, especially Psalm 119:164-172, we see that **reading Scripture always has been bound with prayer**.[3] For example, the Psalmist wrote, "Seven times a day I praise you because your edicts are just … May my lips pour forth your praise, because you teach me your laws. May my tongue sing of your promise, for all your commands are just."

Jesus conversed with the disciples on the road to Emmaus. Failing to recognize Jesus at first, the disciples shared their sadness with Him. Jesus responded by explaining the Scriptures. When "their eyes were opened and they recognized him," they said to each other, "Were not our hearts burning (within us) while he spoke to us on the way and opened the Scriptures to us" **(Lk 24:31-32)**. This burning expressed their personal encounter and deep dialogue with Jesus, one that we can have as well.

POPE BENEDICT AND *LECTIO DIVINA*

Pope Benedict XVI recommends that we make *Lectio Divina* a cornerstone of our lives:[4]

The Church must be constantly renewed and rejuvenated and the Word of God, which never ages and is never depleted, is a privileged means to achieve this goal. Indeed, it is the Word of God, through the Holy Spirit, which always guides us to the whole truth (**cf. John 16: 13**).

In this context, I would like in particular to recall and recommend the ancient tradition of *Lectio divina*: the diligent reading of Sacred Scripture accompanied by prayer brings about that intimate dialogue in which the person reading hears God who is speaking, and in praying, responds to him with trusting openness of heart (**cf. *Dei Verbum*, n. 25**). If it is effectively promoted, this practice will bring to the Church — I am convinced of it — a new spiritual springtime. As a strong point of biblical ministry, *Lectio Divina* should therefore be increasingly encouraged, also through the use of new methods, carefully thought through and in step with the times. It should never be forgotten that the Word of God is a lamp for our feet and a light for our path (**cf. Ps 119[118]:105**).

VATICAN II AND PRAYING SCRIPTURE

The Catholic Church strongly encourages **prayerful** reading and reflection on Holy Scripture:

"Easy access to Sacred Scripture should be provided for all the Christian faithful" and "all the Christian faithful" should "learn the 'excellent knowledge of Jesus Christ' (**Phil. 3: 8**) by frequent reading of the divine Scriptures. (As St. Ambrose wrote) 'Prayer should accompany the reading of Sacred Scripture so a dialogue takes place between God and man. For, we speak to Him when we pray; we hear Him when we read the divine oracles [Scriptures]'" (***Dei Verbum*, Sec. 22 and 25**).

Mass Readings and *Lectio Divina*

Finally, hearing the Word in the Liturgy and reading with prayerful meditation are closely linked and can be the basis for *Lectio Divina*. The Most Reverend Mariano Magrassi, O.S.B. explains the importance of continued prayer and meditation on Scripture before and after the Mass:

> If the soul is conscious of its identity with the mystery with the Church, it will spontaneously rediscover the close link between liturgical hearing and personal meditation. A kind of spiritual exchange will take place. The soul in its moments of prayer will easily remain influenced by what moved it during the liturgy; it will relive it, probe it more deeply, and personalize it in one-to-one dialogue with the divine speaker. On the other hand, what the soul experiences in these moments of prayer will, as it were, flow back to it as it listens during the liturgy. It will be totally present to the reading; it will listen more receptively and be more fully open. The two moments become complementary aspects of a single act.[5]

Part 2

Journaling

"For mental prayer, in my opinion, is nothing else than the intimate sharing between friends; it means taking time frequently to be alone with Him who we know loves us."

ST. TERESA OF AVILA, Doctor of the Church
Catechism of the Catholic Church, 2709

Journaling Deepens *Lectio Divina*

Journaling can be an important part of the prayerful reading of Scripture and practice of *Lectio Divina*. Writing down your experience in the Word of God deepens meditation and prayer. It allows you to go back, review, and admire what God is doing in your life on a daily basis.[6]

There are at least four spiritual benefits to journaling:[7]

1. Journaling aids in the development and articulation of your relationship with God.
2. Journaling helps to uncover unknown thoughts, feelings, and desires of your inner self (e.g., *I didn't know I felt like this or thought this way.*)
3. Journaling provides perspective outside of yourself — that is, God's perspective which includes liberation from racing thoughts that can occupy your mind.
4. Journaling provides an opportunity to look back on your journey with God and experience the blessings, the inner healing, and the answers to prayer all over again.

In summary, journaling as part of *Lectio Divina* helps you express in writing your relationship with the Lord. It helps you uncover your thoughts, feelings, and desires, especially those the Holy Spirit brings to the forefront. It helps you keep a record of your growth, healing, and transformation. Journaling also helps you stay focused on Scripture, reflection, and prayer.

Most of all, journaling helps you capture the blessed moments you spent in dialogue with God. Then, at a later time, you can enjoy, treasure, and even revisit those moments of communion with Him that are especially precious to you. In this return to those same precious moments, also called repetition, you allow God to continue His dialogue with you.

Part 3

The WRAP Acronym

"*Lectio Divina* should be increasingly encouraged, also through the use of new methods, carefully thought through and in step with the times. It should never be forgotten that the 'Word of God is a lamp for our feet and a light for our path' (Ps 119[118]:105)."

POPE BENEDICT XIV
International Congress – September 16, 2005

WRAP: A Guide to
Lectio Divina with Journaling

WRAP is an acronym for a method to guide you through the process of Scripture reading, reflection, and prayer with journaling. Each letter of the word **WRAP** stands for a step in the journaling process. **WRAP** begins after you have chosen a section of Scripture to read prayerfully.

"**W**" stands for **WRITE**.

After you have read the passage that you selected, **WRITE** down a particular verse or verses from that section of Scripture that inspire you or speak to your heart. You will want to underline the word or words to which you are most drawn. St. Philip Neri describes this stage as listening for the words upon which your heart rests. These are the verses that seem to arise out of the passage and capture your attention.

"**R**" stands for **REFLECT**.

Look for the truth (i.e., rule or principle) in the verse or verses you have written, and **REFLECT** upon the truth the Lord is communicating to you. Looking for the truth will help you stay grounded in the meaning of the Scripture passage. Ask Jesus to give you His mind and His thoughts as you meditate on the principle so that you glean what He wants to reveal to you today. As Father Thomas Green, S.J. explains:

> Meditation is reflective searching of the scriptures to discover what God reveals of himself in the person of Jesus, and to learn by analogy how He is speaking in the events of one's own life … It is not merely a reflective historical study … It is an attempt to discover, by means of the life and teaching of Jesus how God is revealing himself through Christ in the events of our lives today.[8]

Keep in mind that meditation is a prayerful quest. According to the *Catechism of the Catholic Church*, meditation "engages thought, imagination, emotion, and desire" (CCC 2708). Thus, you will want to speak to God from your thoughts, feelings, and desires as you contemplate the message and its implication for the way you act, live, and treat others.

In the **REFLECT** step, you may rely not only on your reasoning or analytical faculties, but also on your imagination to visualize a scene from Scripture. In passages where events are described, you might try to imagine yourself as an observer or secondary participant in the scene. Try to reflect on what you hear and see, and to whom you are drawn. Ask yourself: *How am I moved by the scene? What is the Lord telling me?*

> **Note:** Some find it easy to visualize a scene, while others find it easy to analyze the meaning, and still others find both reasoning and imagination helpful. The method that works best for you will depend on your preferences and the passage. In some instances, your Bible footnotes or commentary may further help you understand the scriptural meaning and context.

Write down your conversation with the Lord. Consider the following:
- what you **relate** to Him (your thoughts, feelings, and desires);
- what you **receive** from Him; and
- how you **respond** to Him.

"A" stands for **APPLY**.

In this step, consider how you will **APPLY** the scriptural principle from the **REFLECT** step. Ask Jesus for guidance about what you can do to respond in a concrete or practical way. Keep in mind that the Lord always speaks in love, and His call to follow Him is always extended with great love. Write down the steps you will take to apply His Word to your life today.

"**P**" stands for **PRAY and PRAISE**.

Write a **PRAYER** that offers praise and thanksgiving to the Lord. Praise Him for being your Shepherd, your Healer, and your Companion (or use other praises – see **Appendix**). Thank Him for your moments together. Thank Him for the Scriptures that He brought to you today. Thank Him for speaking to you and loving you. Finally, pray the Scripture verses back to the Lord in your own words, including a response to the dialogue you had with Him today. Try to pray from your heart about what the verses opened in your mind, your emotions, and your life.

For example, invite Jesus to heal you and to touch any hurt or sadness. Invite Him to help you walk in forgiveness. Ask Him for the graces you need to respond in faith to what He revealed to you. Ask Him to help you live out His love toward others. Ask Him to help you memorize the verse to keep in your heart. Write out your prayer and praise.

At the end of your prayer, **stop writing** and **stop speaking**. Focus completely on the Lord. Simply rest with Jesus, close to His heart.

- Enjoy His presence.
- Savor His communion.
- Let Him love you.
- Receive His grace and strength.

Part 4

WRAP Examples

"Whether we realize it or not, prayer is the encounter of God's thirst with ours. God thirsts that we may thirst for Him."

Catechism of the Catholic Church, 2560

Carol's Example: A Verse

The following pages contain examples of **WRAP** sessions to help you understand this method. In the first brief **WRAP**, note how the acronym **W**rite, **R**eflect, **A**pply, **P**ray guided Carol in Scripture reflection and prayer.

Carol began by selecting a daily Mass reading (Acts 2:22-32) to **WRAP**. As she read, verse 26 (Therefore my heart rejoiced and my tongue was glad. Moreover my flesh also will rest in hope.) seemed to arise out of the passage. The words caught her attention. They seemed to invite her to think more about them, and they began to speak to a need of her inner being.

Carol, a cancer survivor, said she constantly worried about when the cancer might come back. The worry seemed to come and go often in the daily routines of her life. When she chose to **WRAP** the Mass reading that day, her thoughts were not on her cancer, but the Lord knew the needs of her heart. Carol **wrote** down the verse. Next, she began to reflect on the words. She invited the Lord to help her see the truth that He was speaking to her.

The words "rejoice" and "rest" from the verses kept coming to mind. As she pondered more, the word "flesh" seemed to speak of her physical health. Insight entered her mind and soul. She realized she was wasting precious time worrying about her "flesh" or her body and the time she would have left on earth. It was as though God was speaking to her inner being and asking her to enjoy each moment He was giving her in her earthly home. One day, she would experience the greatest joy — to be present with Him at His home. So she wrote the truth, "Our future is to be with God in heaven."

Carol's thoughts turned to application, and she wrote: "Don't worry about how much time I have here in this body, but be happy and enjoy each moment."

Finally, she began to dialogue with Christ in prayer. She would need His help and grace to stop worrying and to apply what He was asking of her. She boldly wrote her prayer with thanksgiving: "Dear Jesus, I love you and praise you. Thank you for curing me of cancer. Thank you for our time together. Help me to put aside my worries of the cancer returning and to enjoy each moment with my family and friends that you have given and will give me …"

CAROL'S WRAP WORKSHEET: A VERSE

<u>Date:</u> November 3
<u>Scripture Reading:</u> Acts 2: 22-32

<u>Write (v. 26):</u> "Therefore my heart has been glad and my tongue has exulted; my flesh, too, will dwell in hope." [In other versions, it reads: "Therefore my heart rejoiced and my tongue was glad. Moreover my flesh also will rest in hope."][9]

<u>Reflect:</u> Our future is to be with God in heaven. (Truth)

<u>Apply:</u> Don't worry about how much time I have here in this body, but be happy and enjoy each moment.

<u>Pray and Praise:</u> Dear Jesus, I love you and praise you. Thank you for curing me of cancer. Thank you for our time together. Help me to put aside my worries of the cancer returning and to enjoy each moment with my family and friends that you have given and will give me. Thank you for the peace I feel that when you do call me to you, it will not be a loss but a new life with you. Let me rejoice in each day that I have and wait with hope for when I will be with you. Amen. I REST in your arms of love and listen to your voice.

Ruth's Example: A Word

Ruth had faced times and events in previous months when she was surrounded by others who ridiculed her deep faith in God. When she chose to **WRAP** Psalm 139: 1-18, her thoughts were not focused on her times of frustration, but God knew the needs of her heart.

As she read, verse 14, the word "well" seemed to arise out of the passage and catch her attention — inviting her to think more about it.

Ruth wrote down the verse and underlined the word "well." She invited the Lord to help her see the truth He was speaking to her.

Ruth's WRAP Worksheet: A Word

Date: July 28
Scripture Reading: Psalm 139: 1-18

Write (v. 14): "My very self you knew." [In other versions, it reads: "You know me right well."][10]

Reflect: God knows me well. He made me well. It is well with my soul. It is well with My Lord. (Truth)

Apply: I need to remember God's "well" toward me. When I am discouraged, when I feel unworthy, when I feel alone, when I feel ridiculed, when I feel dissatisfied with my imperfections, I will say, "It is well with my soul. God the Father and God the Son and God the Holy Spirit know me right well. Jesus died for me, for my sins, and for my imperfections. He is Lord, and He loves me. I am well with the Lord Jesus."

Pray and Praise: Dear Heavenly Father, I praise You that You are the "well" of the universe. You made Your creation well. You made me well. You know me well, and You still love me well. Thank you, Lord, for Your "well." Dear Jesus, please give me the grace to receive Your "well" and to always remember that You are with me and know me right well — even in discouragement, even in insults, even when I am let down by others, and even in my own sin and selfishness. Lord, I love You, and I receive Your "well" now. Amen.

Now I rest in the presence of Jesus and commune with Him. I receive His Love, His Grace and His Strength. (At this point, Ruth took time to sit quietly and rest in the Lord's presence and love.)

JOHN'S EXAMPLE: VERSES AND IMAGERY

In the following **WRAP**, John selected and read John 8: 2-11. As he read verses 9-11, the words seemed to come alive. The Scripture invited him to imagine the scene.

John began to visualize the scene. He reread the verses and imagined himself as an onlooker at the event.

John wrote down the verses and invited the Lord to help him see the principles God was speaking to him.

John's WRAP Worksheet: Verses and Imagery

Date: March 27
Scripture Reading: John 8:2-11

Write (v. 9-11): "And in response, they went away, one by one, beginning with the elders. So he was left alone with the woman before him. Then Jesus straightened up and said to her, 'Woman, where are they? Has no one condemned you?' She replied, 'No one, sir.' Then Jesus said, 'Neither do I condemn you. Go, (and) from now on do not sin any more'" **(Verses 9-11 from Jn 8: 2-11 spoken to John).**

Reflect: I see the men dragging the distraught woman, pulling at her limbs and saying to Jesus that she has been caught in adultery. I think to myself, "Where is the man? If they brought the woman to Jesus, where is the man?" Was that their custom or a double standard? Then I see the men pick up some stones to stone the woman, and I hear Jesus ask the men, but not the woman, "Let he who is without sin, cast the first stone." At the same time, I see Jesus writing something in the sand. What is He writing? Their names? Their sins? As I lean in to get a closer look, a strange thing happens to the men. I see the faces of the men change from pride and arrogance to shame. The words of Jesus have pierced their hearts. Their heads drop, and the stones fall from their hands as they realize their own sins. Each man slowly turns and walks away.

   I see Jesus look with tenderness at the woman. "Woman, where are they? Has no one condemned you? She replied, 'No one, sir.' Then Jesus said, 'Neither do I condemn you. Go (and) from now on do not sin any more" **(Jn 8:10-11).**

   No one is left at the scene but Jesus and me. Then, Jesus turns His gaze to me and says, "Neither do I condemn you. Go and sin no more."

For the first time, I realize the connection between love and grace, between repentance and changed actions. The Lord forgives our sins in great love and mercy, but He commands us to sin no more. (Truth)

Apply: Today, I will accept the Lord's forgiveness of all my sins. I will look honestly at myself and ask: "What sin or fault am I ignoring in my own life because I am so busy pointing out the sins of others?" I will give others the same mercy the Lord gives me. Today, I will try to be less critical. Today, by God's grace, I will turn from my sins and sin no more.

Pray and Praise: Dear Heavenly Father, I praise You that You are merciful. Thank You for allowing me to be a part of this encounter with Your mercy. Today, I receive Your mercy. Help me be merciful to others. By Your grace, I want to build up the body of Christ, instead of stoning others with my arrogance and pride. Jesus, I love You and receive Your forgiveness. I will give the same forgiveness to others. Give me wisdom and strength to follow Your example today and every day. Amen.

Now I rest in the presence of Jesus and receive His mercy, His forgiveness, His grace, and His strength. (At this point, John rested in the Lord's presence and love.)

Part 5

Tips for WRAP

"The Apostle [Paul invites us to] think with Christ's thoughts [cf, Phil 2:5]. And we can do so by reading Sacred Scripture in which Christ's thoughts are the Word, they speak to us. In this sense we must practice *Lectio Divina*, we must grasp Christ's way of thinking in the Scriptures, we must learn to think with Christ, to think Christ's thoughts and thus feel Christ's sentiments, to be able to convey Christ's thinking to others."

POPE BENEDICT XIV,
Reflection during the Liturgy of the Hours, October 3, 2005

Questions and Answers

In the next few pages, you will find answers to questions people frequently ask about **WRAP**. In addition, you will find tips to help you get started.

• How Much Time Does WRAP Take?

The wonderful blessing of the **WRAP** method is that you can journal and reflect on Scripture for as long as you like. You can follow this method for as little as 10 minutes or for as long as time permits — even for an hour or more.

• Where Should I WRAP?

You should go to a place where you can be alone to pray and listen to God's Word. Choose a place where you will feel free to speak and enjoy God's presence without distractions.

Some find it helpful to do a **WRAP** prayer as part of their time at Eucharistic adoration. Others find it helpful to sit in the quiet sanctuary after Mass. Still others find it beneficial to go to a quiet room at home where they are undisturbed.

• What Supplies Do I Need for WRAP?

You will need an empty notebook to use as your journal and a pen or pencil. You will also need your Bible (one with footnotes or commentary is often helpful). Keeping a zippered notebook or tote bag that can hold these supplies so you will have them at hand when you are ready to **WRAP** is a good idea. If you **WRAP** frequently at home, you could use a basket or bookshelf to hold your supplies.

• How Do I Select Scripture for WRAP?

You will want to select a passage of Scripture before you begin your **WRAP** session. You could choose a section from a daily or Sunday Mass reading. As Most Reverend Mariano Magrassi points out, there is a close link between Liturgical hearing of the Word and prayerful meditation. The Word proclaimed in the Liturgy and then meditated on in prayer can resonate with each person, "a function of the special and unique plan he has" for each life.[11]

You could choose a Psalm. The Psalms are considered the prayer book of the Catholic Church and make up the Liturgy of the Hours. You could choose a parable, an epistle, or any chapter or section from a book in the Bible. You can find suggested sections especially conducive to **WRAP** in the Appendix at the end of this book.

To prepare yourself for a **WRAP** session, choose a passage in advance — a section of about 5-10 verses works best. Then, place a bookmark in that section in your Bible.

Begin with Prayer and Pause

You should begin your **WRAP** session by approaching it as a time of prayer. Even if you have never prayed alone or outside of a Church service in the past, start by focusing on God's presence. It is essential that you pause from all distractions and activities of your day. Try to put the Lord at the center of your attention and be totally present to Him.

In a posture that is most comfortable to you, settle yourself into quiet and peacefulness. Remind yourself that the Lord is with you. Picture yourself sitting in the Lord's loving, sustaining presence.

Begin your prayer with thanksgiving. Acknowledge that the Lord is with you by saying something simple like the following:

"Heavenly Father, I come into Your presence. Jesus, I know You are here and love me. Thank You, Lord, that I belong to You. Thank you, Jesus, that You want to speak to my heart today through Scripture. Open my heart as I reflect on Your Word. Come, Holy Spirit, and enlighten my mind to Your truth."

Getting Started

Once you have quieted yourself and started with thanksgiving and prayer, open your journal and write the date at the top of the page. Then, write the citation for the passage you are ready to read (e.g., Mt 18: 21-35).

Next, print the letters "W," "R," "A," "P," spreading them out over a page or two. Or you can print and spread out the four words of **WRAP**: Write, Reflect, Apply, and Pray.

You are ready now to open the Bible and begin to read the passage you selected. Read it several times until a word, verse, or verses jump out to you or capture your attention. When that happens, you are ready to begin writing in your notebook.

In summary, **WRAP** involves these four easy steps:

W = Write: Write out the entire verse or verses that speak to you.

R = Reflect: Reflect on the principle or truth that the Scripture is teaching. Use your imaginative and analytical faculties. Write down your thoughts, feelings, and desires in relationship to the Scripture; and dialogue with Jesus.

A = Apply: Consider how Jesus is calling you to apply the truths from Scripture. Write down your response to the Scripture and how you can apply it beginning today.

P = Pray: Write a prayer related to the verses that offers praise and thanksgiving to God. Ask God to help you respond in faith to His Word.

At the end of your prayer, focus completely on Jesus. Rest in His Heart and presence. Receive His strength, His love, and His grace.

Assimilated

Assimilated and Lived Every Day

WRAP will lead you in a personal encounter with our Lord Jesus Christ through Scripture. This personal encounter is what makes "meditation and contemplation different from the knowledge that the theologian or the historian" brings to us, which is, of course, important, too.[12]

Lectio Divina prayer is a "walk toward God" that is meant to be lived out daily.[13]

> The result toward which we tend is not the realization of some plan of growth and development, but the free and gentle utilization of *Lectio Divina* in the service of achieving an encounter with God through His word, listened to, taken to heart, shared, prayed over, contemplated, assimilated and lived in everyday life.[14]

Try It!

Even if you have never prayed with Scripture before or kept a journal, you will find that **WRAP** is an easy and helpful method to learn and practice *Lectio Divina*. You will find that God's Word is truly alive and that God desires to speak to you today.

As you take the time to read His holy Word and to reflect upon its meaning, you can expect to have a personal encounter with your Savior.

Faithfulness to reading and praying the Word of God will change your life!

Part 6

Deeper Still

"[*Lectio Divina*] consists in pouring over a biblical text for some time, reading it and rereading it, as it were, 'ruminating' on it as the Fathers say and squeezing from it, so to speak, all its 'juice,' so that it may nourish meditation and contemplation and, like water, succeed in irrigating life itself. One condition for *Lectio Divina* is that the mind and heart be illumined by the Holy Spirit, that is, by the same Spirit who inspired the Scriptures, and that they be approached with an attitude of 'reverential hearing.'"

POPE BENEDICT XIV,
Angelus, November 6, 2005

Repetition

If you are experiencing communion with Jesus, why move on?

Once you have practiced **WRAP** and experienced a deepening communion with Jesus in the Scriptures, you will want to relish your experience through repetition. Just because you have finished your **WRAP**, you should not presume that the Lord is through speaking to you about that particular verse. Tomorrow or the next day, He may have more to say to you. Respect God's communication with you, and return to that same reflection until you sense that the Lord wishes you to move on.

The process of repetition in prayer can be described as focusing with a zoom lens on those areas of your **WRAP** where your heart was most affected or moved. Returning to them will help you listen in a deeper way to what the Lord wants to say to you.

Repetition begins with re-reading an entry in your WRAP journal. It should flow out of prayer and help you discover where Jesus is calling you, where you are being pulled, or where you are pulling away from cooperating with the Lord. The secret of fruitful prayer is to stay where you are being impressed, where Jesus is touching your heart and speaking to you. Ask yourself:

- What most impressed me?
- What touched my heart?
- What satisfied or disturbed me?
- What should I pray about next?

St. Ignatius further explains: "If I find what I want, there I will rest without being anxious to pass on, until I content myself" (**Spiritual Exercises, 118, #76**). He advises that you use repetition where you felt frightened, depressed, sad, or anxious. Then you can go back and ask questions such as: *Is my anxiety challenging me? What bothered me the most — the event, the scene, Jesus' words, or other text?* Then, you can ask the Lord for His consolation.

For example, maybe a Psalm lifted you up or made you especially conscious of God's presence. Ask the Lord for encouragement.

Maybe an event in Jesus' life or a parable gave you new insight or allowed you to see yourself in a new way. Ask for strength and discernment.

In summary, through repetition, you go back to your own experience of prayer and journaling. You review and relish the experiences where you were affected or moved so that you can dispose yourself to allow the Lord to dialogue and commune more with you.

Acknowledge, Relate, Receive, and Respond to God's Presence

Christian prayer is not something you do, "but is permitting the Trinitarian God to love you." [15]

Repetition can best be understood as deepening your personal communication with God. It is a continuation of prayer based on what God has begun to communicate with you. Keep in mind that "prayer is a personal response to God's presence" and "it means God first makes Himself present to you."[16] Thus, what God wants to say to you is much more important than anything you may have to say to Him.[17] So how should you continue a previous time with **WRAP** using repetition?

Father John Horn, S. J. reaffirms the place to begin when he explains that Christian prayer is not something you do, but is "permitting the Trinitarian God to love you as you acknowledge, relate, receive and respond (ARRR) within your heart to the Holy Spirit's presence, love pursuing you and desiring to communicate with you."[18] He further points out that whenever

Christian prayer is real, it involves your thoughts, feelings, and desires to communicate with Jesus. Consequently, you can use "acknowledge," "relate," "receive," and "respond" verbs to help you deepen your dialogue with the Lord.

ACKNOWLEDGE

Begin repetition prayerfully and peacefully in a quiet place as you would any time when you practice **WRAP**. Acknowledge that God's presence is with you. He loves you and wants to continue speaking with you. Pay attention to the thoughts, feelings, and desires stirring in your heart from your previous **WRAP**.

RELATE

Now begin to relate to Jesus those thoughts, feelings, and desires. Place all of those thoughts, feelings, and desires into the risen, pierced Heart of Jesus, and invite Jesus' presence into everything you have acknowledged. In this way, you begin to present your real needs to Jesus around your **WRAP** verses. Be sure to talk to Jesus in the first person. He desires to move you into deeper communion with Him. You must be real. Try to go beyond speaking only *about* your thoughts, feelings, and desires; instead, speak *from* them to Jesus. Allow yourself to enter into a trust-filled relationship with Him. Now, record in your journal, following the previous **WRAP**, your communication with Jesus around your thoughts, feelings, and desires. For example, you might write:

RELATE
(Based on **WRAP** of Mt 18: 21-35, especially verse 22 where Jesus speaks to Peter about forgiveness and where Peter asks Jesus how many times one should forgive his brother. "Jesus answered, 'I say to you, not seven times but 77 times.'" In my

WRAP prayer, I wrote, "Heal me, and release any anger or bitterness I feel. Restore me. Help me to forget the pain of what was said, to receive the grace of your forgiveness, and to extend that grace to others.)

• **My Thoughts:** I am trying to forgive my brother, as I know the Lord told me in Scripture yesterday. However, he won't speak to me or answer my calls. What can I do?

• **My Feelings:** I am frustrated, and my anger is growing hour by hour.

• **My Desires:** My desire is to get rid of this burden of anger, bitterness, and resentment that I have been carrying. I want to forgive him. Lord, what can I do?

RECEIVE

Next, you need to be patient and silently **RECEIVE** what the Lord wants to say to you. You have already related to Jesus' loving Heart all of the thoughts, feelings, and desires that stirred in your heart from your **WRAP**. Now, wait in childlike trust to receive communication back from Jesus. Be sure to stay attentive to the Lord and to wait in courage, rather than to listen to inner fears that could lead you to withdraw from trusting in God or trying to control the relationship. Simply trust that God is faithful and full of love for you. Jesus' risen, pierced Heart is yearning to console, encourage, enlighten, heal, forgive, and/or repair your heart. Now, record in your **WRAP** journal what consolations you received from Jesus as you entrusted all of your thoughts, feelings, and desires to Him. For example, you might write:

RECEIVE (Based on **WRAP** Mt 18: 22 — see the previous RELATE example.)

• **My Thoughts:** The Lord spoke to my heart that I will not be relieved of my burdens of anger, bitterness, and unforgiveness based on what my brother does or fails to do. My burdens will be lifted only as I take actions toward my brother that express forgiveness.

• **My Feelings:** I feel relieved of my frustration because I know now what I need to do.

• **My Desires:** My desire is to release forgiveness from my heart and to repent of any way in which I have not entrusted my anger to Jesus, since He desires only to console and love me. And, I desire to write a letter to my brother asking for his forgiveness and extending my love to him.

Respond

Finally, after you have received Jesus' love and consolation, you will be ready to respond to Jesus in a humble and honest way. You may respond with joyful rejoicing for encouragement or enlightenment received. OR you may continue to entrust a struggle to Him. OR you may ask for the grace to stand against a sadness or despair that is especially burdening you. OR you may ask for deepened faith to walk in forgiveness toward yourself or others. OR you may resolve to spend more time in His presence to receive His love. OR you may ask for the strength to take the action you know you are called to take. Now, record in your **WRAP** journal how you will respond to the Lord's communication. You can include any of your thoughts, feelings, and desires, as well as any prayer response. For example, you might write:

RESPOND (Based on **WRAP** Mt 18: 22 — see the RELATE and RECEIVE examples on the previous pages.)

• **My Thoughts:** I can forgive my brother. I will follow what the Lord has shown me to do.

• **My Feelings:** I feel consoled and relieved.

• **My Desires:** I will write a letter to my brother tonight and continue to entrust any frustrations to Jesus' Heart.

• **Prayer:** Lord Jesus, I am encouraged that forgiveness does not depend on my brother. I rejoice that the burden is being lifted from me. I receive your grace and strength today. Please give me the words to write to him. Thank you for speaking to me today. Thank you for loving me and forgiving me. I praise You, Jesus. Amen.

In summary, as part of **repetition** and continued dialogue with Jesus based on the Scriptures He brought to your attention in **WRAP**, **acknowledge, relate, receive, and respond** to your risen Lord from your thoughts, feelings, and desires. Jesus' risen, pierced Heart is always yearning to love you and to be with you — to enlighten, to heal, to forgive, and to repair your heart. As you continue to practice **WRAP** and deepen your communication with Jesus, you will grow in childlike trust of your Heavenly Father and receive still more of His consoling, encouraging, healing love.

Appendix

Suggested Scripture Passages to WRAP

To help you begin to **WRAP**, the following Scriptures passages are recommended. Choose any reading, and **WRAP Yourself in Scripture.**

Ps 1 … The path to blessing and happiness
Ps 3: 1-7 … The Lord relieves fear
Ps 4: 4-9 … Trust in the Lord and rest
Ps 5: 11-13 … The Lord is a refuge and shield
Ps 18: 1-4 … The Lord is strength and refuge
Ps 18: 16-36; 40-50 … The Lord gives strength
Ps 19: 1-6 … Creation shows God's greatness
Ps 19: 7-14 … Blessings of Scripture reflection
Ps 23: 1-6 … Trust in your Shepherd; He cares
Ps 27: 1-6 … Confidence in God in times of stress
Ps 34: 1-8; 9-22 … The Lord answers and protects
Ps 37: 1-8; 23-24; 39-40 … Delight in the Lord
Ps 40: 1-5 … The Lord listens; wait for Him
Ps 46: 1-11 … God is a stronghold in trouble
Ps 91: 1-13 … God's protection and care in danger
Ps 95: 1-7… Praise God for His greatness
Ps 100: 1-5 … Enter into His presence with praise
Ps 103: 1-13 … He heals and forgives you
Ps 119:1-16 and 97-112 … God's Word gives direction
Ps 121: 1-8 … The Lord will keep and guard you
Ps 139:1-5 and 13-18 … God knows you intimately
Ps 145: 1-22 … God's faithfulness; He is good to all
Prv 3:1-12 … Wrap yourself in kindness and truth
Prv 5: 1-22 … The pitfalls of immoral living
Prv 16: 1-9 … God directs your steps
Prv 31: 10-31 … Become a worthy woman/wife
Is 40: 10-14 and 28-31 … Gain new strength
Is 43: 2-7 … God calls you by name
Is 58: 1-12 … True sacrifice and fasting helps others
Jer 29: 11-13 … God has a plan for you

Hos 11: 1-4 … God's personal call to you
Zep 3: 15-17 … God sings and rejoices over you
Mt 6: 19-34 … Trust and do not worry
Mt 8: 23-27 … Jesus calms the storm
Mt 14: 22-33 … Jesus walks on water
Mt 25: 1-13 … Keep your light burning
Lk 1: 26-38 … The Annunciation — Gabriel, Mary
Lk 1: 39-56 … The Visitation — Mary and Elizabeth
Lk 2: 1-20 … The Nativity
Lk 5: 1-9 … Jesus is in your boat; be obedient
Lk 7: 40-48 … The woman who ministered to Jesus
Lk 10: 38-42 … Jesus visits Martha and Mary
Lk 11: 1-13 … Jesus teaches about prayer
Lk 12: 22-32 … Jesus tells the cure for anxiety
Lk 15: 11-32 … God loves the prodigal
Lk 24: 13-35 … On the Road to Emmaus with Jesus
Jn 2: 1-11 … The Wedding at Cana — do what He tells you
Jn 3: 15-21 … God's salvation from sin
Jn 4: 1-26, 39 … The woman at the well
Jn 15: 1-8; 9-17 … Jesus calls you friend — abide
Jn 20: 1-18 … Jesus appears and calls Mary's name
Jn 20: 19-29 … Jesus helps the doubting
Jn 21: 15-19 … Jesus reinstates
Acts 9: 1-20 … Paul's conversion and healing
Rom 8: 31-39 … Receiving Jesus' healing love from which nothing can separate us
Eph 1: 3-14 … Spiritual blessings
Eph 3: 14-21 … God's abundance
Eph 6: 10-18 … Put on God's armor
Phil 4: 1-9 … Keys to peace; pray and be thankful
1 Thes 5: 1-11 … Be vigilant
2 Thes 1:1-12 … Bright hope of Christ's return
2 Tm 4: 1-8 … Share God's Word
2 Pt 1: 1-15 … Guidance for growth in faith
Rv 4: 1-11 … A glimpse of heaven

Scriptural Names of the Trinity for WRAP
Father, Son, and Holy Spirit Praises

God, The Creator of All Things, Praise You. Gn 1:1
God, The Everlasting One, Praise You. Gn 16:13
God, The Most High, Praise You. Gn 14:18
God, The Almighty One, Praise You. Gn 17:1
God, The Great I AM. Praise You. Ex 3:14

Lord of Hosts, Praise You. 1 Sm 1:3
Lord, our Provider, Praise You. Gn 22:14
Lord, our Banner, Praise You. Ex 17:15
Lord, our Peace, Praise You. Jgs 6:24
Lord, our Sanctifier, Praise You. Ex 31:13
Lord, our Righteousness, Praise You. Jer 23:6
Lord, our Healer, Praise You. Ex 15:26
Lord, our Shepherd, Praise You. Ps 23:1
Lord, our Companion, Praise You. Ez 48:35

Jesus, The Son of the Most High, Praise You. Lk 1:32
Jesus, The Son of God, Praise You. Mk 1:1
Jesus, The Son of Abraham, Praise You. Mt 1:1
Jesus, The Son of David, Praise You. Mt 1:1
Jesus, The Son of Mary, Praise You. Mt 1:16
Jesus, The Son of Man, Praise You. Mt 17:22
Jesus, The Bread of Life, Praise You. Jn 6:35
Jesus, The Light of the World, Praise You. Jn 8:12
Jesus, The Gate for the Sheep, Praise You. Jn 10:7
Jesus, The Door to Eternal Life, Praise You. Jn 10:9
Jesus, The True Vine, Praise You. Jn 15:1-5
Jesus, The The Good Shepherd, Praise You. Jn 10:11
Jesus, The Resurrection and the Life, Praise You. Jn 11:25
Jesus, The Way, the Truth, and the Life, Praise You. Jn 14:6
Jesus, The Word Made Flesh Who Dwelt Among Us, Praise You. Jn 1:14
Jesus, The Lamb of God, Praise You. Jn 1:29

Jesus, **The Savior of the World**, Praise You. Lk 1:47
Jesus, **The Man of Sorrows Acquainted with Grief**, Praise You. Is 53:3
Jesus, **The Source of Peace**, Praise You. John 14:27
Jesus, **The Messiah, Son of the Living God.** Praise You. Mt 16:16
Jesus, **The Cornerstone of the Household of God**, Praise You. Eph 2:20
Jesus, **The Name Above Every Name**, Praise You. Phil 2:9
Jesus, **The Image of the Invisible God**, Praise You. Col 1:15
Jesus, **The Head of the Body, the Church**, Praise You. Col 1:18
Jesus, **The Beginning, the First Born from the Dead**, Praise You. Col 1:18
Jesus, **The One Mediator between God and Men**, Praise You. 1 Tm 2:5
Jesus, **The Judge of the Living and the Dead**, Praise You. 2 Tm 4:1
Jesus, **The High Priest**, Praise You. Heb 3:1
Jesus, **The Searcher of Minds and Hearts**, Praise You. Rev 2:23
Jesus, **The Lion of the Tribe of Judah**, Praise You. Rev 5:5
Jesus, **The King of Kings and Lord of Lords**, Praise You. Rev 19:16
Jesus, **The Alpha and the Omega**, Praise You. Rev 21:6

Holy Spirit, **The Spouse of Mary**, Praise You. Mt 1:18
Holy Spirit, **The Breath of the Almighty**, Praise You. Job 33:4
Holy Spirit, **The Convicter of Sin**, Praise You. Jn 16:8
Holy Spirit, **The Giver of Power and Boldness**, Praise You. Acts 1:8
Holy Spirit, **The Giver of Wisdom and Understanding**, Praise You. Is 11:2
Holy Spirit, **The Giver of Counsel and Strength**, Praise You. Is 11:2
Holy Spirit, **The Giver of Knowledge and Fear of the Lord**, Praise You. Is 11:2
Holy Spirit, **The Bearer of Love, Joy, and Peace**, Praise You. Gal 5:22
Holy Spirit, **The Bearer of Patience and Kindness**, Praise You. Gal 5:22
Holy Spirit, **The Bearer of Generosity and Faithfulness**, Praise You. Gal 5:22
Holy Spirit, **The Bearer of Gentleness and Self-Control**, Praise You. Gal 5:23
Holy Spirit, **The Spirit of the Living God**, Praise You. 2 Cor 3:3
Holy Spirit, **The Spirit of Grace**, Praise You. Heb 10:29
Holy Spirit, **The Spirit of Truth**, Praise You. Jn 16:13
Holy Spirit, **The First Installment of our Inheritance**, Praise You. Eph 1:14
Holy Spirit, **The Helper in our Weakness**, Praise You. Rom 8:26
Holy Spirit, **The Interceder for us in Prayer**, Praise You. Rom 8:26
Holy Spirit, **Our Comforter**, Praise You. Acts 9:31
Holy Spirit, **Our Advocate**, Praise You. Jn 14:16

WRAP Guide:
A Cut-Out Reference

On the next page, you will find a **WRAP** Guide, including tips on how to get started. The guide can be cut out or copied and then taped in the first few pages of your **WRAP** journal.

In the brief **WRAP** Guide example provided, verse 22 of Matthew 18: 21-35 spoke to the person doing the **WRAP**. If you would **WRAP** this section of Scripture, you might find that the Holy Spirit would speak to your heart and mind from a different verse in the passage.

WRAP Guide: Getting Started

1. **Collect materials**: Notebook, Bible, pen or pencil.

2. **Choose a quiet place.** Choose a place where you can pray and enjoy God's presence without distractions.

3. **Select a passage of Scripture in advance.** Place a bookmark in that section in your Bible.

4. **Focus on God's Presence.** Settle yourself into peacefulness. Remind yourself that the Lord is present with you. Picture yourself sitting in the Lord's loving, sustaining presence.

5. **Begin with thanksgiving and prayer.** Affirm that the Lord is with you. "Heavenly Father, I come into your presence. Jesus, I know You are here and that You love me. Thank You, Lord, that I belong to You. Thank you, Lord, that You want to speak to my heart today in Scripture. Come, Holy Spirit, open my heart to truth …

6. **Journal.** Record the date and Bible passage you are reading (e.g., Mt. 18: 21-35).

7. **Print.** "W," "R," "A," "P," or spread out the four words represented by **WRAP**: Write, Reflect, Apply, Pray.)

8. **Read.** Open the Bible, and read the selected passage several times until a **word, verse,** or **verses** capture your attention. Begin **WRAP**.

WRAP Yourself in Scripture Guide

W: **Write.** Write down the key verse or verses.

R: **Reflect.** Reflect on the rule (Principle or Idea), and record what God speaks to your mind and heart.

A: **Apply.** Write out how you can apply the message beginning today.

P: **Pray.** Praise the Lord. Pray the verse; make it your own; talk with Jesus. Ask for His grace and help to walk out His Word. Rest in His presence and receive His grace.

EXAMPLE

Pray: (Offer thanks, and ask Jesus to speak to your heart and mind. Ask the Holy Spirit to inspire and guide your study.)

Date: _____   Scripture: Matthew 18: 21-35

W: v. 22 (Jesus speaks to Peter about forgiveness) "Jesus said to him 'I do not say to you, [forgive] up to seven times, but up to 70 times seven.'"

R: There is no limit to forgiveness — forgiveness is essential for a Christian. The Lord has called me to forgive others just as He forgives me.

A: Today, I need to forgive _____

P: Praise and thank you, Jesus, that you died for me and that You forgive all of my sins. Dear Lord, help me to forgive _____for the hurt done to me. Heal me, and release any anger or bitterness I feel. Restore me. Help me to forget the pain of what was said, to receive the grace of your forgiveness, and to extend that forgiveness to others. Amen.

I rest in Your presence and love.

WRAP Worksheet

Date:
Scripture Reading: Psalm 139: 1-18

Write (v.____):

Reflect:

Apply:

Pray:

Rest in His presence and receive His love, His grace, and His strength.

WRAP Worksheet

Date:
Scripture Reading: Psalm 139: 1-18

Write (v.____):

Reflect:

Apply:

Pray:

Rest in His presence and receive His love, His grace, and His strength.

Reference List

"Meditation engages thought, imagination, emotion, and desire. The mobilization of faculties is necessary in order to deepen our convictions of faith, prompt conversion of our heart and strengthen our will to follow Christ. Christian prayer tries above all to meditate on the mysteries of Christ as in *Lectio Divina* or the rosary. This form of prayerful reflection is of great value, but Christian prayer should go further; to the knowledge of the love of the Lord Jesus, to union with him."

Catechism of the Catholic Church, 2708

Endnotes

[1] Father Sam A. Morello, O.C.D., *Lection Divina and the Practice of Teresian Prayer* (Washington, D.C.: ICS Publications, 1995).

[2] Ibid.

[3] Father Dominic F. Scotto, *Liturgy of the Hours* (New York: Catholic Book Publishing, 1987).

[4] Pope Benedict XVI, International Congress on *Dei Verbum* (September 16, 2005).

[5] Most Rev. Mariano Magrassi, O.S.B., *Praying the Bible: An Introduction to Lectio Divina* (Collegeville, Minnesota: The Liturgical Press, 1998), 9-10.

[6] Very Rev. Rodrigo Polanco, "Spiritual Formation as the Core Which Unifies and Gives Life to Seminary Formation: One Seminary's Experience," in "Interiority for Mission: Spiritual Formation for Priests for the New Evangelization," Rev. Richard J. Gabuzda, *Fourth Symposium on the Spirituality and Identity of the Diocesan Priest* (Omaha, Nebraska: The Institute for Priestly Formation, 2005).

[7] J. Alkire, *Healing: Stories of Faith, Hope, and Love* (St. Paul: Paulist Press, 2003).

[8] Father Thomas H. Green, S.J., *Opening to God: A Guide to Prayer* (Notre Dame, Indiana: Ave Maria Press, 2006), 102.

[9] Carol used the *New American Bible and Notes (NAB)*, St. Joseph Edition, 1970.

[10] Ruth used the *New American Bible and Notes (NAB)*, St. Joseph Edition, 1970.

[11] See Magrassi, *Praying the Bible*, 7.

[12] See Green, *Opening to God*, 104.

[13] Mario Masinai, *Lectio Divina: An Ancient Prayer That Is Ever New* (New York: Alba House, 1998), 99.

[14] Ibid., 100.

[15] Father John Horn, S.J., *Heart Speaks to Heart: A Review of Life and Healing Prayer* (Omaha, NE: The Institute for Priestly Formation, 2009), 28.

[16] Father Armand Nigro, S.J. *Praying with Scripture*, 1.

[17] Ibid.

[18] See Horn, *Heart Speaks to Heart*, 28.

Works Cited

Alkire, J. *Healing: Stories of Faith, Hope, and Love*. St Paul: Paulist Press, 2003.

Benedict XVI (2005). Make 'Lectio Divina' a cornerstone of your life. In *L'Osservatore Romano: Vatican*, September 21.
Available: Http://www.vatican.va/holy_father/benedict_xvi/speeches/2005/september/documents/hf_ben-xvi_spe_20050916_40-dei-verbum_en.html (December 8, 2008).

Catechism of the Catholic Church (CCC). New York: Doubleday, 1995.

Green, Father Thomas. H., S. J. *Opening to God: A Guide to Prayer*. Notre Dame, Indiana: Ave Maria Press, 2006.

Horn, Father John, S. J. *Heart Speaks to Heart: A Review of Life and Healing Prayer*. Omaha, Nebraska: The Institute for Priestly Formation, 2009.

Magrassi, Most Rev. Mariano, O. S. B. *Praying the Bible: An Introduction to Lectio Divina*. Collegeville, Minnesota: The Liturgical Press, 1998.

Masinai, Mario, Professor. *Lectio Divina: An Ancient Prayer That Is Ever New*. New York: Alba House, 1998.

Morello, Father Sam A., O.C.D. *Lectio Divina and the Practice of Teresian Prayer*. Washington, D.C.: ICS Publications, 1995.

New American Bible and Notes (NAB), St. Joseph Edition, 1970.

Nigro, Father Armand, S. J. *Praying with Scripture*.

Polanco, Very Rev. Rodrigo. "Spiritual Formation as the Core Which Unifies and Gives Life to Seminary Formation: One Seminary's Experience." In Richard J. Gabuzda (Director), *Fourth Symposium on the Spirituality and Identity of the Diocesan Priest.* "Interiority for Mission: Spiritual Formation for Priests for the New Evangelization." Omaha, Nebraska: The Institute for Priestly Formation, 2005.

Scotto, Father Dominic F. *Liturgy of the Hours.* New York: Catholic Book Publishing, 1987.

St. Augustine. *Sermo de Nativitate Domini.*

St. Ignatius. *Spiritual Exercises*, 118, #76.

Turks, Father Paul. *Philip Neri: The Fire of Joy.* New York: Alba House, 1995.

Vatican Council II. *Dei Verbum.*

Vatican Council II. *Gaudium et Spes.*

Vatican Council II. *Lumen Gentium.*